Pastoral Care
& Holistic Ministry

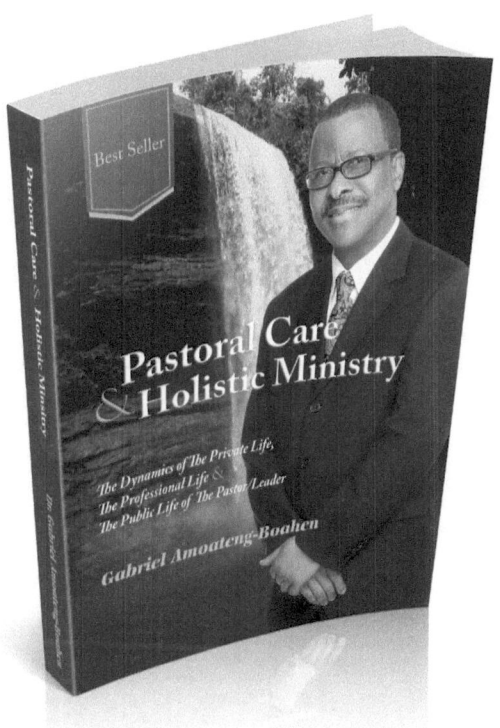

Dr. Gabriel Amoateng-Boahen

Mrs. Agatha Amoateng-Boahen

Pastoral Care And Holistic Ministry

All Rights Reserved

Copyright © 2016 by Gabriel Amoateng-Boahen

No part of this publication may be reproduced, stored in a retrieval system or transmitted in any way by any means, electronic, mechanical, photocopy, digital imaging, recording or otherwise, without the prior written permission of the author who is the copyright owner, except as provided by USA copyright law.

Bible references are taken from the various translations of the Bible as stated.

Author's Contact: *gabriel.ab925@yahoo.com*
gabrielabm1913@gmail.com

First Printed in July 2016

The opinions expressed by the author in this book are not necessarily those of Rehoboth House.

EBook: ??????
Paperback: 978-1-68411-021-6
Hardcover: ?????

Published in the United States of America by
Rehoboth House, Chicago.
www.*rehobothhouseonline.com*

Table of Contents

Dedication..xiii
Acknowledgment...xv
Preface..xvii
Abstract..xix
Introduction..xxi

Chapter 1
The Private Life of The Pastor/Leader..................................1
Enjoy Spiritual Direction From God..2
The Ministry Must Be Sustainable...3
The Health of the Pastor..4
Enjoy Family Support...5
Strategic Time Management..5
Travailing and Prevailing in Prayer..8
The Study Life of the Pastor...10
Appreciate and Bless Others...10
Choose Your Words Judiciously...11
Be an Encourager to Somebody Else.......................................13
Create a Self-Sacred Space...14
Prayer...16

Chapter 2
The Professional Life of The Pastor/Leader.........................17
Develop the Culture of Excellence in Your Life and Ministry.....22
Have Compassion for People and Passion for Ministry..........22
Do Not Muddle Up Things Together......................................23
Keep Inventory of the Ministry..23
Have Excellent Knowledge of Logistics...................................24
Encourage "Spiritual Division of Labor".................................24
Have Regular Scheduled Meetings With Your Leaders..........25
Avail Yourself for Critical Feedback in Humility....................26
Do Not Cloud Your Call or Vision..28
Time Alone with God...29
Word from God..30

Chapter 3
The Public Life of The Pastor/Leader 33
Handle Your Complexed Network of Relationships Prayerfully 33
Be Close but Distant Yourself in Public 34
Observe Pulpit Ethic 34
Avoid Unnecessary Competition and Egocentrism 35
Join Professional Associations with Other Ministers 36
You Are Heaven's Ambassador 36
Be an All-Round Public Figure 37
You Are a City On a Hill 38
Network with Other Minsters and Ministries 39

Chapter 4
The Counseling And Support Needs of The Pastor/Leader:
Who Pastors The Pastor? 41
Human Weaknesses of the Pastor/Leader 41
Locate Your Spiritual Mentor 43
We Grow Through Trials and Challenges 44
The Pastor/Leader is a Blessing to the Society 45
Marriage and Family Matters and Ministry 47
Individual Roles in the Family in Relation to Ministry 48
Family Life is Integral and Cardinal to Effective Ministry 52
Business to Support Ministry and Accompanying Challenges 52
Justification for the Pastor to Be Pastored 53

Conclusion 55

Author's Profile 57

Recommended Books 71

Author's Prayers For Readers 75

Dedication

Dedicated to the Erbowor-Becksen family (James, Ernestina, Alfred, Zita, and Carl). Without each other we are nothing.

Dedication

Acknowledgment

"... There are "friends" who destroy each other, but a real friend sticks closer than a brother" (Prov.18:24, NLT).

The above theme verse captures my heart cry. This is a "Sacred and Divine Moment" to appreciate all my old and new Christian Brothers and Sisters scattered all over the world especially, those in Ghana, US, and London for your continued support diversely. Your support is phenomenal, cohesive, and amazing. Hand in hand we support each other on our respective journeys to Heaven. Without each other we are nothing.

The same appreciation is extended to all Pastors, Ministers, and Church Leaders, and the entire Body of Christ as we always bear in mind that we are One Big Family with a Common Father God, Jesus Christ our Brother, and the Holy Spirit our Friend.

Acknowledgment

Preface

According to Encyclopedia of Christianity, Pastoral Care is the ministry and counseling provided by pastors, chaplains, and other religious leaders to members of their church and congregation, with a focus on healing, reconciling, guiding, and sustaining. Pastoral Care is broader than what most people imagine.

Ministry is simply service by the pastoral caregiver to God's People everywhere at any given time. The services are sacrificial, challenging, but rewarding, and therefore, there is the need to create a peaceful, pastoral, congenial, and "sacred space and time" for both the caregiver and receiver. This is necessary for effective pastoral care ministry.

It takes Divine Grace filled with love, compassion, and passion to companion the hurting and the heart-broken. The word holistic connotes wholeness, totality, all-embracing, and all- fulfilling.

The book first and foremost focusses on the private, professional, and public lives of the pastoral caregiver- pastors, church leaders, chaplains, counselors, psychotherapists, and others. For effective pastoral ministry, and to nail down and address the core issues bothering the individual, the caregiver looks beyond the ordinary and superficial but journeys into the deep with the counselee, mentee, or directee. In other words, the caregiver looks for the pertinent and disturbing issues emanating from the body, soul, and spirit of the receiver of pastoral care.

> **"May God himself, the God of peace sanctify you through and through. May your whole spirit, soul, and body be kept blameless until our Lord Jesus Christ comes again" (1 Thess. 5:23, NIV).**

These three areas of the human person are intrinsically intertwined and interwoven, too complex and delicate to separate one from the other. This is to say that there is always a chain of reaction closely knitted together that is too difficult to divide when one is affected or infected, hence the need for professionals to handle the individual competently and confidently (body/physical- health professionals like doctors, nurses, and others); soul/mind/emotions- counselors, chaplains, psychotherapists, and others); and spirit- pastors, priests, spiritual directors, spiritual leaders, and others).

The professional listens pastorally, critically, compassionately, passionately, and empathetically to identify the real problem ("the shadow" side of the predicament/pathology) to be able to get to the root cause through the empowerment, inspiration, and presence of the Holy Spirit.

Turning down the volume of our busy lives allows the pastoral caregiver to listen to God for Divine Direction which leads to powerful, fruitful, effective, and abiding Pastoral Care and Holistic Ministry. This is a point of emphasis and worthy of notice by all Ministers of the Gospel/Pastoral Caregivers.

Abstract

According to Encyclopedia of Christianity, Pastoral Care is the ministry and counseling provided by pastors, chaplains, and other religious leaders to members of their church and congregation, with a focus on healing, reconciling, guiding, and sustaining. Ministry is simply service by the pastoral caregiver to God's People everywhere at any given time. The services are sacrificial, challenging, but rewarding, and therefore, there is the need to create a peaceful, pastoral, congenial, and "sacred space and time" for both the caregiver and receiver. It takes Divine Grace filled with love, compassion and passion to companion the hurting and broken-hearted. The word holistic connotes wholeness, totality, all-embracing, and all-fulfilling. Turning down the volume of our busy lives allows the pastoral caregiver to listen to God for Divine Direction which leads to effective Pastoral Care and Holistic Ministry.

Abstract

Introduction

People have various perceptions of the life of the pastor, depending on their previous experiences with pastors and the church as the Body of Christ. These perceptions form the basis of their expectations of the pastors' life. Consequently, they relate to them based on those preconceived views they hold.

In this book, we are going to discuss four aspects of the pastor's life. (1) The Private Life of the Pastor. (2) The Professional Life of the Pastor. (3) The Public Life of the Pastor, (4). The Counseling and Support Needs of the Pastor - Who Pastors the Pastor?

What is pastoral care and holistic ministry? It is the ministry of care and counseling administered by pastors, chaplains and other spiritual leaders to members of their church or congregation, with a focus on healing, reconciling, guiding and sustaining. Ministry is simply, service by the pastor or leader to God's people everywhere at any given time. It is sacrificial and challenging. Those of us who have been in ministry for some time will agree with me that it is indeed sacrificial. At times, even your money has to be involved for the ministry to move forward.

Introduction

Sometimes we cry quietly in private when things are not going well. There are certain things we can't share publicly, but as ministers and leaders we commune with the Lord quietly in prayer. My fervent prayer and hope is that you remain resolute and never be discouraged in any form for responding positively to the Call of God upon your life. Ministry as I said, is service by the pastor or leader to God's people everywhere at any given time. No doubt, it is a sacrificial and challenging assignment.

May the Lord grace you to have grace and compassion for people and passion for the ministry He has committed to your trust.

In my book, Spiritual Mentorship for Pastors and Church Leaders Today, I wrote briefly about being compassionate for people and passionate for ministry. I want you to note these two phrases, compassion for people, and passion for ministry. As we progress further, I will expound more on them.

Ministry becomes sour, distasteful, lack of spiritual energy and motivation, when we lose the passion for ministering and the initial enthusiasm that propelled us to launch out in faith when we first responded to the call. We become very sad, very emotional, very un-motivational about the very call that once upon a time we responded passionately with enthusiasm. In other words, the calling upon the individual's life now becomes a burden rather than a joy. At that point, he/she dangles like a pendulum, being tossed like the wave of the sea, not knowing whether to retreat, move forward or to quit.

> "Therefore, my beloved brethren, be steadfast, immovable, always abounding in the work of the Lord, knowing that your labor is not in vain in the Lord' (1 Cor. 15:58, NKJV).

I wrote this book as a source of encouragement to us as ministers to find grace and move forward to the glory of God. You will agree with me that one of the most unpleasant ministerial experiences is to lose your passion for ministry. Lack of motivation renders ministry routine and ritualistic. In our routine, we do the same thing day in day out, all through the week, the month, and the year. Life and ministry become ritualistic and a mere form of godliness without the power to authenticate our ministry. We can predict, when we start from here, we are going to end there. Sadly, so we do every day, every week, every month, every year, and for years we have been doing almost the same thing without tangible and lasting impact to attest our ministry.

> **"And say to Archippus, "Take heed to the ministry which you have received in the Lord, that you may fulfill it" (Col. 4:17, NKJV).**

Brothers and sisters, men and women of God, the time has come for us to really wake up from slumber and embrace the power of the Holy Spirit in us to really energize and propel us to the next level to the glory of God.

> **"And do this, knowing the time, that now it is high time to awake out of sleep; for now, our salvation is nearer than when we first believed. The night is far spent, the day is at hand. Therefore, let us cast off the works of darkness, and let us put on the armor of light. Let us walk properly, as in the day, not in revelry and drunkenness, not in lewdness and lust, not in strife and envy. But put on the Lord Jesus Christ, and make no provision for the flesh, to fulfill its lusts" (Rom. 13:11-14, NKJV).**

However, the question remains, "Who pastors the pastor"?

Introduction

CHAPTER 1

The Private Life Of The Pastor/Leader

From the pastoral care standpoint, let's examine the private life of the pastor in relation to healing, reconciling, guiding, and sustaining. Because of the high expectations people have for pastors, many people do not realize that pastoral care among other things aims at healing, reconciling, guiding, and sustaining. So in talking about holistic pastoral care ministry in reality, we are discussing the physical aspect of the pastor's life, the soul aspect or the emotional aspect of the pastor and as well as the spiritual aspect of the pastor's life. The church member, counselee, mentee, or directee (pastoral care receiver) like the pastor (pastoral caregiver), equally has physical, emotional, and spiritual needs. The ministry becomes holistic when the pastor takes serious cognizance of all three needs (physical, emotional, and spiritual) of the members. In sum, the word holistic applies to both the caregiver and receiver.

There is need for self-reconciliation in order to experience holistic pastoral care. The pastor must ensure that he/she remains reconciled with God and help members to do likewise. This is very important. It is common today in our society to see people angry with themselves.

If you are angry with yourself as a pastor or a leader, inadvertently, you will transfer the same aggression to people around you and the innocent church members who come to church to listen to the Word of God. So as a leader you must first reconcile yourself. In other words, just come to terms with God. Probably some of us are still carrying baggage from the past that is affecting our ministry today. We must resolve not or allow our past to deter our future, but rather press on towards the glorious future God has for us as pastors and leaders. Let us learn from Apostle Paul.

> **"Brethren, I do not count myself to have apprehended; but one thing I do, FORGETTING THOSE THINGS WHICH ARE BEHIND and reaching forward to those things which are ahead, I press toward the goal for the prize of the upward call of God in Christ Jesus" (Phil.3:13-14, NKJV).**

Enjoy Spiritual Direction From God

As pastors and leaders of God's people, we must pay the price required to enjoy spiritual direction from God. These days some pastors and church leaders, though not all, wake up in the morning and whatever comes to their mind they announce in church and it becomes a spiritual policy, which everybody is expected to adhere to. My brothers and sisters, we must endeavor to hear the voice of God. If we are going to make any major move in our churches, in our fellowships, in our small or big ministries, and the larger society, we must hear the voice of God and enjoy the spiritual direction from Him. As a leader of God's people, you don't arbitrarily do things on your terms and comfort. Let God speak to you and direct you on what He wants done. This is a very important aspect in ministry that we all need to take note of.

The Ministry Must Be Sustainable

Here I am talking about sustainability. There are people who with enthusiasm started something with joy and zeal, after a period of time they vanish from the scene. Either they abandon that noble cause or become irrelevant in the things of God. Though they may be around, you don't feel the impact of their ministry. Whatever God is calling you to do must be vibrant and sustainable. Sustainability in ministry is key in holistic ministry. Therefore, holistic ministry must be sustained by the glory of God and to the glory of God.

If you are reading this book, I believe that God has brought this timely message across to you at the right time. The Bible says, buy the truth and sell it not. In other words, value and preserve the things you are reading in this book.

> "Buy the truth, and do not sell it, also wisdom and instruction and understanding" (Prov. 23:23, NKJV).

Jesus demonstrated and taught sustainability as an example for us to emulate in Luke 9:62,

> "And Jesus said unto him, no man having put his hand to the plough and looking back is fit for the kingdom of God". So my brothers and sisters, now that we have touched the work of God, it is required that we continue till the end. This is what we call no turning back.

> "Being confident of this very thing, that He who has begun a good work in you will complete it until the day of Jesus Christ: (Phil .1:6, NKJV).

Yes, we must keep moving forward till we finish the race, and be ready to receive the reward at the end.

> "For I am already being poured out as a drink offering, and the time of my departure is at hand. I have fought the good fight, I have finished the race, I have kept the faith. Finally, there is laid up for me the crown of righteousness, which the Lord, the righteous Judge, will give to me on that Day, and not to me only but also to all who have loved His appearing" (2 Tim. 4:6-9, NKJV).

Let me draw your attention to this fact. When you see soldiers well dressed in their military outfit, in most cases they don't have cover at their back. According to Ephesians chapter six description of our spiritual armor, there isn't much at the back. The implication is that when you are enlisted in this army, you keep advancing until you enter heaven. We must adopt the no retreat no surrender attitude, with an unwavering faith to sustain our respective ministries to the glory of God who is able to help us complete what He began.

The Health of the Pastor

Pastors, your health is only second to your salvation. Therefore, devote quality time for self-care. You see some ministers, and right away you know that they are physically exhausted and worn out. Most times we blame the devil for everything. If you are tired you must rest. This is not the work of the devil. Yes, if you are tired, I say you must rest. It's as simple as that. So just deliberately create time for yourself. Even God rested after creation on the seventh day. The best person to guarantee the effectiveness of a product and how to maximize the potential of that product is the manufacturer. The concept of rest was introduced into the human life by God-the maker of mankind. It will be tantamount to foolishness if we violate this law and not expect the consequence.

> "By the seventh day God had finished the work he had been doing; so on the seventh day HE RESTED FROM ALL HIS WORK. And God blessed the seventh day and made it holy, because on it he rested from all the work of creating that he had done" (Gen. 2:2-3, NIV).

Jesus too, rested after the day's ministry. He observed the law of rest and was very effective in His ministry here on earth.

> "The apostles gathered around Jesus and reported to him all they had done and taught. Then, because so many people were coming and going that they did not even have a chance to eat, he said to them, "Come with me by yourselves to a quiet place and get some rest" (Mark 6:30-31, NIV).

Enjoy Family Support

The pastor must enjoy family support. We all need family members to support us in ministry. So let's put premium on family life, husband, wife, children, biological, adopted, and Christian sons and daughters, grandchildren, and other members. It's so important because in our most difficult moments they are the very people to comfort and encourage us.

Strategic Time Management

Plan your schedule and maximize every passing second because time is ministry and ministry is time. Endeavour to tithe one tenth of your 24 hours, which is 2 hours 40 minutes. That gives us a rough idea about the amount of time we need to spend with the Lord each day, at least. I have a pastor friend far away in Ghana, at times he calls me, Chicago time, around 2:00 am and tells me that for the last three hours he has been praying. And then somebody would ask, what should I be praying for, for about three hours or more? Brothers and sisters, if you really want to pray and start praying, you can be engaged in it for up to four hours or more. Unfortunately, because the zeal is lacking in many of us today even as pastors and leaders, when we start praying, after 5 to 10 minutes, we are tired and ran out of prayer burden and points. The motivation to pray is not there any longer. This is the time to reawaken ourselves out of every form of spiritual slumber and allow the Spirit of God to move us to the next level in life and ministry.

> **"Awake, you who sleep, arise from the dead, And Christ will give you light." Walk in Wisdom. See then that you walk circumspectly, not as fools but as wise, redeeming the time, because the days are evil. Therefore, do not be unwise, but understand what the will of the Lord is" (Eph. 5:14-18, NKJV).**

Prayer gives birth to ministries and vibrantly sustains them. Jesus in the gospel of Luke.

> **"Then He spoke a parable to them, that men always ought to pray and not lose heart" (Luke 18:1, NKJV).**

Resolve to tithe one tenth of your time daily in study and prayer with the Lord. God is calling us to redeem lost times because the days we are living are encumbered with evil. He gave us the responsibility to redeem the time because these are evil days and the love of many is waxing cold like Jesus said.

> "And because lawlessness will abound, the love of many will grow cold. But he who endures to the end shall be saved. And this gospel of the kingdom will be preached in all the world as a witness to all the nations, and then the end will come" (Matt. 24:12-14, NKJV).

You have the responsibility to redeem your own time. We spend eight hours sleeping and another eight hours working, all things being equal. Therefore, your precious gift is today. We have only today to live and express the life and gifts God endowed us with, to be a blessing to others. Tomorrow will always be in the future. The most important and relevant time anyone has is now. What you do with your today ultimately impacts your tomorrow. Leave no room for "African Punctuality." In order to effectively manage our time, we must consciously avoid any form of distractions in ministry. Give your time to bless others. Why? Because it is more blessed to give than to receive.

What do you do with your last 8 hours? All things being equal, we spend the first 8 hours sleeping to rest, the second 8 hours working. What you do with your last 8 hours, which some call leisure time, matters very much. Great inventions, new discoveries, and many books were written during the last "inventive and creative" 8 hours.

> "In everything I did, I showed you that by this kind of hard work we must help the weak, remembering the words the Lord Jesus himself said: 'It is more blessed to give than to receive'" (Acts 20:35, NIV).

Distractions In Ministry

Let me give you a practical example of what I am meant by avoiding distractions in ministry. My daughter and I were trying to arrive in good time to a meeting where I was the guest speaker, and in the process we locked ourselves. At that point I realized this was a distraction. Interestingly, it was a special day to me, because I was coming with joy and enthusiasm to meet servants of God and discus kingdom matters. The first question that came to mind was how do I enter my room after the conference? I told her that this was a distraction and consciously ignored the thought. We have to be sensitive to discern distractions when they come or else we capitulate to them. Distraction can dissuade you from God's plans for you.

Whenever you are being distracted as a man or woman of God, shove the distraction aside and focus on what God is calling you to do. Distractions come in many forms. At times they may come from your spouse, children, coworkers, colleagues in ministry even your best friends, immediate or extended families, business partners, name it. You may have ten minutes to a preaching engagement and then somebody calls you on the phone and tries to throw all the preaching overboard. At such times, be resolute, push it aside and focus on the assignment ahead of you. You can always return to talk with the fellow. In my scenario, if I was to concentrate on the key and how to get into to my room after the conference, I couldn't have been able to keep my appointment to speak to the pastors and church leaders at the Southside of Chicago - organized by Bishop Odell Thompson Sr., Stratford Christian Center Church, 9152 South Ashland Avenue, Chicago, Illinois, 60620, USA. We must focus on what God has called us to do, regardless of what confronts us. Jesus on His way to Jerusalem set His face like a flint.

Travailing and Prevailing in Prayer

I'm talking about the Hezekiah type of prayer that reversed potential death to life. It's the kind of prayer that you labor till you prevail.

> "In those days Hezekiah became ill and was at the point of death. The prophet Isaiah son of Amoz went to him and said, "This is what the Lord says: Put your house in order, because you are going to die; you will not recover." Hezekiah turned his face to the wall and prayed to the Lord, "Remember, O Lord, how I have walked before you faithfully and with wholehearted devotion and have done what is good in your eyes." And Hezekiah wept bitterly" (2 Kings 20:1-3, NIV).

Jesus' prayer at the Gate of Gethsemane is a classic example of the need to travail and prevail in prayer.

> "On reaching the place, he said to them, "Pray that you will not fall into temptation. He withdrew about a stone's throw beyond them, knelt down and prayed, Father, if you are willing, take this cup from me; yet not my will, but yours be done. An angel from heaven appeared to him and strengthened him. And being in anguish, he prayed more earnestly, and his sweat was like drops of blood falling to the ground" (Luke 22:40-44, NIV).

My daughter in London is a professional midwife and an occupational therapist. To the glory of God, she is also a minister of the Gospel. She recently wrote a book on "Spiritual Labor Room: Travailing and Prevailing in Prayer." Mothers can easily identify with this reality because of their experiences in the labor room at the time of delivery. Every woman that has given birth to a child went through labor, though at various degrees. The rule is that, labor precedes delivery. Using this metaphor to illustrate the spiritual parallel between travailing in prayer and travailing in labor as a woman, reveals the crucial nature and urgency for travailing and prevailing in prayers as ministers of God. The Bible says that as soon as Zion travails she brought forth her child.

> "Who hath heard such a thing? who hath seen such things? Shall the earth be made to bring forth in one day? or shall a nation be born at once? for as soon as Zion travailed, she brought forth her children" (Isa. 66:8, KJV).

There are depths we cannot experience and accomplish in ministry without travailing and prevailing in prayers, hence the need for this dimension of prayer can't be over emphasized nor substituted.

The Study Life of the Pastor

Though it has been proven overtime that studying worth the effort at all stages of life. As pastors and leaders, we can't afford to compromise our study life. It is the bedrock upon which the Lord can build ministries through our lives. It also gives us divine validation and better equips us for kingdom service. If studying has a premium value in our everyday life, I am convinced it's more valuable in our spiritual life and walk with the Lord.

> "Study to shew thyself approved unto God, a workman that needeth not to be ashamed, rightly dividing the word of truth" (2 Tim. 2:15, KJV).

Study is simply building capacity both for ministry and everyday life. The more knowledgeable you are, the more resourceful you are. You can't give what you don't have. If God instructs us to study, then we have to place high premium on our study life as minsters.

Appreciate and Bless Others

Research shows that compliments boost you and those you compliment. One of the earnest desires of the human nature is the craving for appreciation. Everybody wants to be valued and recognized for who they are and for what they have accomplished in life. When as pastors and leaders we express our appreciation to others, it helps build and in some cases rebuild their worth and self-esteem. There is a positive influence that erupts within any recipient of genuine appreciation (emphasis on genuine appreciation because these days we have all kinds of appreciations in the system. The very people who appreciate you turn around to gossip about the same appreciation). It creates a sense of value and worth. The more often we appreciate people the more value we help them build and consolidate. Typically, appreciation is an added value to the recipient and also to the one who appreciates. Let us therefore endeavor to be the blessing we are called to be.

"I will make you into a great nation and I will bless you; I will make your name great, and you will be a blessing" (Gen 12:2, NIV).

William James, well-known psychologist and philosopher, said, **"The earnest principle of human nature is a craving to be appreciated."** If people are convinced that you are interested in their wellbeing, they will be naturally drawn to you. It enhances their overall impression of you and evokes an unquestionable loyalty. Be frank with them and don't flatter.

Choose Your Words Judiciously

It is necessary to understand how the nature and the dynamics of words impact everyday life. The power of spoken words cannot be over emphasized. They have the ability to heal or to harm, to kill or to make alive, to encourage or to discourage, to inspire or to despair, to uplift or to downcast. **"Words are alive. Cut them and they bleed."** - Ralph Waldo Emerson. What we say can make a lasting impact on people.

> "Death and life are in the power of the tongue, and those who love it will eat its fruit" (Prov. 18:21, NKJV).

As pastors and leaders, we are required to choose our words with great caution, because it can either make or mar our hearers. The Scriptures explicitly say;

> "Let your speech always be with grace, seasoned with salt, that you may know how you ought to answer each one" (Col. 4:6, NKJV).

Words are crucial to life so much that God exalted His word above His name as an example for us to emulate.

> . "… For You have magnified Your word above all Your name" (Psalm 138:2, NKJV).

As ambassadors of God's heavenly kingdom, we are required to be worthy representatives of our home country by words and actions. The words we speak should impart grace to the hearers. I have chosen to use four different translations of the Bible to expound deeper the message embedded in Ephesians 4:29.

> "Don't use foul or abusive language. Let everything you say be good and helpful, so that your words will be an encouragement to those who hear them" (Eph. 4:29, NLT).

> "Don't say anything that would hurt another person. Instead, speak only what is good so that you can give help wherever it is needed. That way, what you say will help those who hear you" (Eph. 4:29, GWT).

> "Let no harmful language come from your mouth, only good words that are helpful in meeting the need, words that will benefit those who hear them" (Eph. 4:29, CJB).

> "Do not let any unwholesome talk come out of your mouths, but only what is helpful for building others up according to their needs, that it may benefit those who listen" (Eph. 4:29, NIV).

We have been ordained as oracles of God to bless and not to curse. Therefore, our choice of words is crucial to the success of our individual and collective ministries God has entrusted us with.

Be an Encourager to Somebody Else

As the distractions and pressures of the society increase in an alarming rate, people are becoming more self-centered, consequently encouraging others is almost a lost art today. As pastors and leaders we should not be caught in the web of self-centeredness and neglect our responsibility of encouraging others.

> "We sent Timothy, who is our brother and God's fellow worker in spreading the gospel of Christ, to strengthen and encourage you in your faith, so that no one would be unsettled by these trials. You know quite well that we were destined for them" (I Thess. 3:2-3, NIV).

One of the attributes and responsibilities of the believer irrespective of office or position is to be an encourager to others. There is need for us to consciously find time to give courage to those who are discouraged, especially as pastors and leaders.

> "Therefore, encourage one another and build each other up, just as in fact you are doing" (1 Thess. 5:11, NIV).

Encouragement goes a long way to uplift the spirits of a discouraged brother or sister who may be experiencing some sort of a trial. Today, we just get too busy to be concerned about the welfare of our fellow human beings, and busyness becomes an excuse for neglecting them. As Christians, we must find the time to be concerned about others, about their welfare, about their happiness, and about their spiritual growth! We are our brother's keeper. We should not be like Cain who did otherwise.

> "Then the Lord said to Cain, "Where is Abel your brother?" He said, "I do not know. Am I my brother's keeper?" (Gen. 4:9, NKJV).

Encouragement goes a long way to boosting the spirits of a discouraged friend who must persevere through a trial.

> "So this weak brother, for whom Christ died, is destroyed by your knowledge. When you sin against your brothers in this way and wound their weak conscience, you sin against Christ. Therefore, if what I eat causes my brother to fall into sin, I will never eat meat again, so that I will not cause him to fall" (1 Cor. 8:11-13, NIV).

Create a Self-Sacred Space

In theology you would call it, powerful, personal, pastoral presence. This is to create a cordial welcoming space to receive your counselee. You must be fully present to give your fullest attention to hear the brother/sister in front of you. Cell phones and other distracting gadgets must be muted to connote seriousness and readiness for your pastoral care receiver. This is allowing the Spirit of God to take hold of you so much that when people who are hurting come in contact with you, God begins to minister healing to them through your life – that is the presence of God you radiate. As you step up to preach, people are comforted and encouraged. We must carry the pastoral presence wherever we go.

> **"As a result, people brought the sick into the streets and laid them on beds and mats so that at least Peter's shadow might fall on some of them as he passed by. Crowds gathered also from the towns around Jerusalem, bringing their sick and those tormented by evil spirits, and all of them were healed" (Acts 5:15-16, NIV).**

This presence emanates from our consistent fellowshipping with the Lord in worship, prayer, mediation, and studying. Just time alone with God will cause His presence to rob off on you. Therefore, expressing God's presence through your life is crucial to the success and impact of your ministry.

This is an excerpt from Our Daily Bread of February 18, 2016, and I am quoting to emphasize the need for public service, solitude with Jesus, and physical rest for our weary bodies as ministers who work around the clock 24/7.

"When Jesus began His public ministry of teaching and healing He was catapulted into the public eye and throng by people seeking help. Crowds followed Him wherever He went, right? But Jesus knew that having regular time alone with God was essential to maintaining strength and perspective."

"After Jesus' 12 disciples returned from their successful mission to proclaim the kingdom of God and to heal the sick He took them to a quiet place to rest." "Luke 9:2, soon however crowds of people found them and Jesus welcomed them. He spoke to them about the kingdom of God and healed those who needed healing. Instead of sending them away to find food, the Lord provided an outdoor picnic for 5,000 people. Jesus was not immune to the pressures of curious and hurting people but He maintained the balance of public service and solitude by taking time for rest and for prayer alone with His Father." We need to create that balance.

PRAYER

"Dear Father, as Jesus your son and our Lord and Savior honored you in solitude and service to others, may we follow His example in our lives."

We need to create that balance. Turning down the volume of life allows you to listen to God (emphasis is mine). That's very powerful. The volume of this life is so loud that we need to consciously turn it down to be able to listen to the voice of God.

CHAPTER 2

The Professional Life of the Pastor/Leader

It's unrealistic to talk about professionalism without anchoring it to work ethic. These twin components are bedfellows necessary to succeed in ministry as a pastor/leader and typically in every other endeavor in life. The word 'professionalism' has been defined diversely. An example from "Houston Chronicle" defines it as; 'a strict adherence to courtesy, honesty and responsibility when dealing with others. One of the key elements of professionalism is a high level of excellence, above and beyond the basic requirements of whatever you do. Work ethic refers to personal values expressed in the process of discharging your duties and imparting the same values across the ministry or organization.

You can agree with me that inculcating professionalism in ministry is crucial to the success and height the ministry can attain. With the above definition, it is obvious that the most professional being in the universe is God. Let's look at the key words that define professionalism in the light of the Scriptures.

> Courtesy: "Finally, all of you be of one mind, having compassion for one another; love as brothers, be tenderhearted, be courteous; (1 Peter 3:8, NKJV).

From the above Scripture, it is evident that God requires us to be courteous in our dealings with people. Courtesy requires us to be selfless, respectful, and considerate to others. When we are courteous as required by God, it enables us to see things from the perspective of others as well. One key element of courtesy that is most consistent with the character of God is selflessness.

> **"... But because of his great love for us, God, who is rich in mercy, made us alive with Christ even when we were dead in transgressions — it is by grace you have been saved" (Eph. 2:1-6).**

Evidently, being courteous can help build one's reputation as a merciful and thoughtful person, who thinks of the interest of others, even when it hurts him. The selfless sacrifice of His son Jesus was a demonstration of God's selfless concern for others.

> **Honesty: "You shall do no injustice in judgment, in measurement of length, weight, or volume. You shall have honest scales, honest weights, an honest ephah, and an honest hin: I am the Lord your God, who brought you out of the land of Egypt" (Lev. 19:35-37, NKJV).**

The book of Leviticus is a compendium of legal, ceremonial and the morale codes of God. This divine code of conduct was given to Israel at a time in their life when God was transforming them from being a mob of slaves into becoming one of the greatest nations in human history. This code of ethics was intended to become the governing principles of their everyday life in relation to one another, the surrounding nations and God who brought them out of the Egyptian enclave and manacles of slavery. As they were transiting from a mob of slaves to a self-governing nation, they needed a constitution to guide their daily living in the Promised Land.

There are many Scripture references to honesty we can further study to accentuate the point I am stressing here about the importance of honesty in the professional life of the pastor/leader.

From the above Scripture, it is evident that God requires us to maintain a high level of honesty when dealing with others. **"No legacy is so rich as honesty"** - William Shakespeare. Wikipedia refers to honesty as "a facet of moral character and connotes positive and virtuous attributes such as integrity, truthfulness, straightforwardness, including straightforwardness of conduct, along with the absence of lying, cheating, theft, etc. Furthermore, honesty means being trustworthy, loyal, fair, and sincere." The more honest you are, the more your reputation soars and brings more glory to God.

> *Responsibility*: "And say to Archippus, see that you discharge carefully [the duties of] the ministry and fulfill the stewardship which you have received in the Lord" (Col. 4:17, AMP).

Responsibility in this context as a pastor or leader, refers to "a duty or obligation to satisfactorily perform or complete a task at the scheduled time (assigned by someone, or created by one's own promise or circumstances) that one must fulfill, and which has a consequent penalty for failure" as defined by an online business dictionary. In talking about professionalism in pastoral ministry, it's imperative to come to terms with the reality of our divinely assigned responsibility over the lives of the people the Lord - the Chief Shepherd has committed to our trust and jealously guard them.

Jesus demonstrated a perfect example for us to follow, as accounted in John chapter 17 when He was giving His report to the Father who assigned Him the job. He perfectly executed His assigned duty. He knew that in stewardship, faithfulness is required.

> "I have revealed you to those whom you gave me out of the world. They were yours; you gave them to me and they have obeyed your word. .... While I was with them, I protected them and kept them safe by that name you gave me. None has been lost except the one doomed to destruction so that Scripture would be fulfilled" (John 17:6-12, NIV).

He knew the scope of His responsibility and was careful to function within the parameters of His assignment. He told His Father that, He has kept everyone given to Him, except one (Judas) that the Scripture might be fulfilled.

Professionalism requires that your duties be well defined and precise to the point, until you are redeployed by your employer. In this scenario as a pastor/leader, your ministerial boundaries have to be obviously defined by the Lord. Look at Paul recounting in Acts 26 how he was commissioned by the Lord Jesus Christ in Acts 9, on his way to Damascus.

> "But rise and stand on your feet; for I have appeared to you for this purpose, to make you a minister and a witness both of the things which you have seen and of the things which I will yet reveal to you. I will deliver you from the Jewish people, as well as from the Gentiles, to whom I now send you, to open their eyes, in order to turn them from darkness to light, and from the power of Satan to God, that they may receive forgiveness of sins and an inheritance among those who are sanctified by faith in Me" (Acts 26:12-18).

The other form of responsibility is the one created by you. It's a personal commitment you made to help you effectively discharge your assigned duties. At this point you don't renege from your promises. You do everything possible within your capacity to ensure that your word counts. Consequently, creating a trust around your life and ministry that people begin to count on you. King David gives us a typical example and reveals how this attitude can strengthen our personal relationship with God.

> "Lord, who may abide in Your tabernacle? Who may dwell in Your holy hill? ... He who swears to his own hurt and does not change" (Ps. 15:1-4, NKJV).

> Excellence: "O Lord, our Lord, how excellent is Your name in all the earth" (Ps. 8:9, NKJV).

Basically speaking, excellence has been defined by many as the quality of being outstanding or extremely good (the best) in whatever you do. Obviously, excellence has been defined diversely. But one thing that is common in all definitions across board, is the word best in all ramifications. Excellence cannot be anything less than best in all ramifications. Obviously, it is an attribute of God.

> "As for the Almighty, we cannot find Him; He is excellent in power, in judgment and abundant justice; He does not oppress" (Job 37:23, NKJV).

One of our brothers who demonstrated professional excellence in his political service even as a prophet of God was Daniel. He was impeccable to the point of becoming an influence and a reference point in Babylon. Amazingly, even till today he is being spoken of.

Develop the Culture of Excellence in Your Life and Ministry

Developing the culture of excellence in your life and ministry naturally puts you on the path to success. As pastors and leaders of God's people, optimizing the use of every available resources within your ministry can engender excellence. Our relationship with God the most excellent, is a viable resource when it comes to cultivating and demonstrating professional excellence in ministry. This one-on-one relationship should be guarded jealously. Ministers that consciously strive for excellence usually exceed normal performances and achieve sustainable and outstanding results. In most cases they become the standards and reference points. They lead as role models. In order to sustain their accomplishments, and possibly accomplish greater heights, they constantly seek for opportunities to improve at whatever level they are. Often time, they come up with innovative ideas and divine inspiration, because of their commitment to excellence and variant relationship with the Lord, in prayer, study and fellowshipping.

Have Compassion for People and Passion for Ministry

Don't confuse the two, compassion for people and passion for ministry. Without these two key ministerial qualities functioning in your life, very minimal can be accomplished. If you lose passion for ministry, it becomes a routine and a drag. If you lose compassion for people, you become insensitive to their needs and concerns. Jesus is a perfect example of a compassionate pastor. Listen to what He said to His disciples, teaching them to do likewise after His departure.

"I have compassion for these people; they have already been with me three days and have nothing to eat. If I send them home hungry, they will collapse on the way, because some of them have come a long distance" (Mark 8:2-3, NIV).

Do Not Muddle Up Things Together

Consciously have a work schedule and calendar for meetings and strictly follow it, unless otherwise directed by the Holy Spirit. The Scripture tells us in Acts 13 and 2 to *"Separate unto me Barnabas and Saul..."* The Holy Spirit is the master planner and scheduler. Even when you have made a plan you must still be dependent on the Holy Spirit to direct you on what to do, how to do it, and when to do it. It is imperative to inculcate strategic planning into ministry, but under the guidance of the Holy Spirit.

Keep Inventory of the Ministry

Have all the necessary basic equipment —digital cameras, videos, computers, and other multimedia devices to enhance proper recording of events of the ministry, for the present and next generation. Some of us have ministered powerfully in time past and experienced the presence and manifestation of God's power as people received instant miracles. But today, personally I have no documented evidence, either electronically or otherwise to show to my children, who are also actively engaged in global ministry as international conference speakers. This ought not to be so, especially as technology advances.

The Billy Graham Classic at the Trinity Broadcasting Network (TBN) is there to tell us to put our powerful sermons and preaching together in whatever form available to you for the next generation. Inventory helps you to keep track and plan effectively. It helps you know what you need and what you have at each time. It also helps you to know when to do additional purchases or do necessary upgrades to catchup with merging technologies, in order to meet the growing demands of the 21st century ministry.

Get the necessary basic office stationery and desk supplies, needed to professionally run the day-to-day activities of your ministry readily available, —letterheads, envelopes, business cards, to mention a few. It is shocking that some of us literally struggle to locate a business card. As simple an ordinary as it sounds, it is unprofessional and must intentionally be avoided with every caution. Note, what is applicable to you may not be to the next person, probably because of office environment or other peculiarities. Go for what is necessary and peculiar to your ministry

Have Excellent Knowledge of Logistics

As general overseers, pastors, and ministry leaders, you should have an excellent knowledge of whatever goes on in the ministry. Follow up with all delegated assignments. Some leaders delegate and never follow through to ensure execution. Consequently, the same issues still linger unresolved, without any change, thereby impeding productivity. This is unprofessional and should be consciously avoided at every instance.

Encourage Spiritual Division of Labor

Do you know that division of labor is an economic model that the business world has used for centuries? Amazingly, this is God's leadership model. Moses used it when he was pastoring a whole nation. As a leader, encourage spiritual division of labor and do not try to do it all by yourself. Make adequate use of the human resources the Lord has brought your way.

> "Moreover you shall select from all the people able men, such as fear God, men of truth, hating covetousness; and place such over them to be rulers of thousands, rulers of hundreds, rulers

of fifties, and rulers of tens. And let them judge the people at all times. Then it will be that every great matter they shall bring to you, but every small matter they themselves shall judge. So it will be easier for you, for they will bear the burden with you. If you do this thing, and God so commands you, then you will be able to endure, and all this people will also go to their place in peace" (Exod. 18:21-23, NKJV).

Tiredness limits the anointing upon your life and impacts your health negatively. I can assure you that if we adhere to these Kingdom principles, at least it will really put our lives together and enable us do the work effectively to the glory of God.

Have Regular Scheduled Meetings With Your Pastors/Leaders

As you schedule regular meetings with your leaders, ensure to follow proper meeting procedures and protocol. Encourage each department head to give a brief report of the status of their department for critique and evaluation, and possibly make suggestions for improvement. Your goal as the leader is to encourage and inspire every leader to maximize their God-given potentials. However, be strict but friendly, and above all, be very caring, loving, and professional. The business world has much to teach us in this aspect, let us learn in humility. I salute the business men and women reading the book. They always attempt to maximize every time they have, whether they are travelling or on vacation, they attempt to take full advantage of the time. Let us translate the same mentality and ideals into the house of God and into the ministry. In closing, give the "State of the Ministry" address and summarize the reports and activities of all the sub-ministries and set new goals.

Avail Yourself for Critical Feedback in Humility

Genuine feedback is a performance-improvement mechanism. If you have not been doing it, please consider inculcating it into your life and ministry. Again, the business world beats us here. In some cases, they pay to get reviews, feedbacks and surveys. With some of us, whatever we do is right and we don't want anybody to give us any opinion, or feedback. When you do that you don't grow in ministry. Avail yourself for critical feedback in humility. Remember that Jesus washed the feet of His disciples as an example of humility for us to emulate. Humility is a virtue that has to be covetously cultivated.

> "After that, He poured water into a basin and began to wash the disciples' feet, and to wipe them with the towel with which He was girded" (John 13:5, NKJV).

Avoid unnecessary justification and explanation. Rather, be less defensive. Naturally, our first human reaction or instinct is to defend our point of view, intellectually and "legally" (avoid being a "defense attorney"). Let us all follow the classic example of our Lord and Savior, Jesus Christ.

> "Let this mind be in you, which was also in Christ Jesus. Who, being in the form of God, thought it not robbery to be equal with God: But made himself of no reputation and took upon him the form of a servant, and was made in the likeness of men" (Phil. 2:5–7).

Let me share a practical example. When I came from Ghana to further my education in America, I wasn't computer literate at the time. I had problem with accent, I had problem with food, I had problem with almost everything trying to assimilate into a new culture. My peers in the first school attended were all white that grew up in this culture. I was the only black man in the class struggling to adapt to my new environment. They will be making fun of me that I am computer illiterate even as an adult. As they gave me very blunt and pointblank feedbacks, I was documenting them as resource materials, adding them to what I have learned. At the end of the semester, I will have grade A and they will have grade B.

So over the years, my brothers and sisters, to the glory of God, I have grown through responding accordingly to pointblank feedbacks. In ministry, if you really want to see visible results and impact, just sit back and allow people to give you honest feedback, because iron sharpens iron in ministry.

"As iron sharpens iron, so one man sharpens another" (Prov. 27:17, NIV).

It's your responsibility to decipher the genuine feedback from false accusation designed to shoot you with the arrow of criticism and condemnation. You should know people who are genuine and honest. There are some people whatever you do is good, don't go near them. Yes, whatever you do they will tell you, oh, you did great, you did great! And then at your back they will give their negative feedback and criticize you on everything. That is not kingdom practice.

"It is better to correct someone openly than to have love and not show it" (Prov. 27:5, NCV).

Do Not Cloud Your Call or Vision

Do not for anything whatsoever cloud God's calling upon your life, with even relevant issues that are not related to the ministry He has entrusted to your stewardship. Stay focused and e in tune with the Holy Spirit on a daily basis. Unfortunately, some men and women of God are trying to surrogate the ministry God has given them with other business concerns. Please understand and don't get me wrong. I'm not against doing business alongside your ministry. We must know the dividing line. We need to know which one takes precedence over the other. Whatever you do to support the ministry, I encourage it, provided it does not clash and subjugate the higher calling of serving Jesus and His people as a minister. Apostle Paul was actively a business person as well as one of the most influential ministers of the Gospel ever lived, because he kept his priorities right and focused on his core assignment.

> "After Athens, Paul went to Corinth. That is where he discovered Aquila, a Jew born in Pontus, and his wife, Priscilla. They had just arrived from Italy, part of the general expulsion of Jews from Rome ordered by Claudius. Paul moved in with them, and they worked together at their common trade of tentmaking" (Acts 18:1-3, TMB).

There are people in our various congregations God has anointed to do exploits in the business world. We must discover them and train them for that Kingdom assignment, even though they may have been trained in best Business Schools of the world. They still need divine impartation to conquer in the battle of the marketplace. Men and women of God, make no mistake, Babylon is still active in business world doing everything possible to defile us, but God wants to beat and consecrate their gain and their substance to expand His Kingdom on earth before the glorious return of the Lord.

> "...Arise and thresh, O daughter of Zion; For I will make your horn iron, And I will make your hooves bronze; You shall beat

in pieces many peoples; I will consecrate their gain to the Lord, And their substance to the Lord of the whole earth" (Mic 4:10-13, NKJV).

All my five biological children are actively in full time ministry. Concurrently, they are doing other things to support their ministries. I have no problem with that. I am also in active ministry and in a situation where they are trying to go overboard, then I raise the red flag. Your ministry must be your prime concern and then the business supporting your ministry. Take note, your first ministry is you ministering to the Lord; that is your personal devotional life. Then your family is the second ministry before ministering to people. Unfortunately, this divine order has been neglected and distorted over the years by some ministers. The time to reevaluate our priorities has come. We should linger no further.

> "He must be a good family leader, having children who cooperate with full respect. If someone does not know how to lead the family, how can that person take care of God's church?" (1 Tim. 3:4-5, NCV).

Time Alone with God

Cultivate a sustainable practice of periodic retreat from the rowdiness of ministry. Ministry can be rowdy as you deal with issues and people. Jesus, after ministering to the people would retreat to spend time alone with the Father and then empowered for the next assignment.

> "And when He had sent the multitudes away, He went up on the mountain by Himself to pray. Now when evening came, He was alone there" (Matt. 14:23, NKJV).

When you retreat and retire in God's presence, you are re-fired to re-strategize for the next level. You know that the Gospel is the same unchangeable Word of God, universally. But why is it that when some people preach, it comes with such a penetrating power that invigorates, convicts, energizes, rekindles hope and unspeakable joy in the lives of people? But others when they preach, it's just like a mere motivational talk that excites the emotions of the hearers. We need to retreat and retire in God's presence to be re-fired for greater heights in ministering to people.

Notice in the business world, if a company is not making profit they don't continue to lose, instead they reevaluate their performance and business strategies, and ask pertinent questions why they are losing. They realize that they need to restructure their operations and re-strategize in order to make profit the next time.

A Word from God

Wait on the Lord to receive a message on behalf of His people. The days of storytelling in church are gone. Your pulpit must be holy and sanctified with edifying words. Do not infuse any personal issues into your preaching. Find time to deal with personal issues in the church before or after church. If you preach a "personal message" from the pulpit, a radical member will respond from the congregation personally. The pulpit is for God's people and not your "courtroom." Do not "airlift" another pastor's message for your congregation because the audience is different. A different audience needs its own message at a specific time, depending on what is going on with them either individually or corporately. Read books of other men and women of God to enrich your message and your life. Pastors, please, never underrate your members.

All things being equal, the spirituality of the pastor dictates the spirituality of the church and ministry. Quantitatively, if the spirituality of the pastor or leader is 8 on a scale of 1–10 (10 being the highest), no member will have a spirituality of 9 under your leadership. You cannot give what you don't have.

The Professional Life of the Pastor/Leader

CHAPTER 3

The Public Life of the Pastor/Leader

The public life of the pastor is crucial in changing our society for the better. Like I have said in my book on "Spiritual Mentorship," I strongly believe that if our communities and the globe at large is going to get better, God is counting on the pastors and ministry leaders to influence the change in their respective communities, through their ministries and the relationships with the public. The Church is a vehicle of change, so are our lives and ministries.

> "Let your light so shine before men, that they may see your good works and glorify your Father in heaven" (Matt 5:16, NKJV).

Handle Your Complexed Network of Relationships Prayerfully

Handle your complex network of relationships prayerfully, carefully, diplomatically, and thoughtfully. When delegating one of your leaders to deputize for you, if possible, write your speech and ask whoever is deputizing to read and explain it. These days, human beings are becoming very complex, so if you are asking your minister to go and deputize for you, write the speech or at least provide an outline for him. Chances are that the individual may say things you did not ask him to say. It's advisable to write your speech, if possible, sign and put the final full stop and give to the leader to go and read on your behalf. In God's work, we should not leave things loose and give the enemy an opportunity to betray and ruin what God has built through our lives and ministries over the years. He can influence and lure the people we have trusted to destroy the ministry. As long as we are in the flesh, we are vulnerable to the temptations, but by the help of the Holy Spirit, we can overcome.

> "For in that He Himself has suffered, being tempted, He is able to aid those who are tempted" (Heb. 2:18, NKJV).

Be Close but Distant Yourself in Public

This is a paradoxical statement. Be close but deliberately distant yourself in public. Pray for the wisdom to handle this. I cannot give a formula but pray and ask God to give the wisdom to navigate through it. I say, be close to people but at the same time distant yourself from them. Familiarity breeds contempt.

Observe Pulpit Ethic

Respect other ministers' pulpit whenever you go to minister. Sincerely, go with the mind of Christ to add but not to subtract. Some ministers go to other people's church, and they end up creating confusion after ministering. When they leave, some people leave the church. It is not a good spirit. Please, whenever you have the opportunity to minister as a guest, ask God to use you to bless the congregation and the ministry that gave you the privilege. You must respect and honor the man or woman of God and the leadership of the ministry. You must take instructions from the authority of the ministry. You should not do or say anything to destroy the reputation of the pastor, the leadership and the ministry. Desire to add to whatever they have been building over the years. Let nothing be done through selfish ambition or vain glory but in lowliness of mind let each esteem the other better than themselves, according to Philippians 2:3.

Avoid Unnecessary Competition and Egocentrism

Ministers should avoid unnecessary competition and egocentrism when they meet for community events. If you are called to minister after the main speaker, try not to destroy what the previous speaker built while ministering, rather build on it. When you disparage their ministration, you are not adding to the Body of Christ. Understand and respect the individual ministry gifts God endowed us with. Focus on what God has called you to do at the time.

My four sons are all prophets with strong prophetic accuracy. They will look at your face and tell you almost every detail about your life from your date of birth, depending on what the Lord wants to accomplish at that material time through their prophetic ministries. God uses them mightily across the globe, even to minster to presidents of nations. That is the type of children God has blessed me with. I don't envy them, but rather thank God for their lives. But there is one thing they cannot take from me, my position as their father. On that premise, they cannot compete with me. So I give them critical feedback. While I was writing this book (February 2016), Prophet Sampson was on his way to Birmingham-UK, he ministered in Memphis, Tennessee before he left for Birmingham.

Sometimes I even miss their names. Prophet Daniel and Dr. Mark were in Ghana ministering, while Prophet Brian was ministering in Cincinnati, Ohio, my daughter Veronica was also ministering in London and of course, Sister Christabel, the upcoming little prophetess was in Chicago with me. So what is the point? Don't envy the other ministers. Focus on what God has called you to do.

Join Professional Associations with Other Ministers

As you join the professional network of ministers, be humble to learn what you don't know. Don't claim to know it all. For me, the more I learn, the more I realize how much I don't know and how much I need to know. It takes a humble heart to admit this fact and resolve to learn. These days some pastors and leaders are all over the places claiming to know everything. As you sit back and hear them minister, you puzzle if they are preaching from the same Bible we all have. They go off tangent, almost preaching heresy.

You Are Heaven's Ambassador

Remember that you are representing the Kingdom of Heaven as an ambassador. Your disposition affects your church, your ministry, your family, your community, and your nation. In view of this fact, comport yourself respectfully even when you are emotionally pushed to the wall. Let me give you a practical example. I went to minister with a minister friend as guest speakers. To the glory of God, under the influence of the Holy Spirit, my friend ministered powerfully at the program. After the ministration, a young man confronted and disrespected us, and we held our peace. Shortly afterwards, this same young man aggressively confronted us again attempting to evict us from the rented place my friend and I were staying. We were emotionally pushed to the wall. Unfortunately, my friend was not sensitive enough to discern the enemy was at work, so he reacted and the glory of the ministration quickly dissipated within seconds because some of the people we had ministered to were still around and could not believe my friend could easily go overboard. To add fuel to the burning flame, "the emotional button pusher' said to my friend" you call yourself a preacher and look at your behavior in public" Indeed, his comment was the last straw that broke the camel's back.

"Now then, we are ambassadors for Christ, as though God were pleading through us: we implore you on Christ's behalf, be reconciled to God" (2 Cor 5:20-21, NKJV).

When you are being pushed to the wall emotionally as a man or a woman of God, get yourself together and know that the enemy is at work. You saw how within seconds after ministration, all the fasting, the prayers, the preparation, and the powerful ministration evaporated into thin air.

Be an All-Round Public Figure

Have a fair knowledge of what goes on in your community and respond accordingly as able. Community involvement opens more doors of opportunities for ministry. Don't isolate yourself from the community where your ministry is located. Get involved in the life of the community but don't be part of them and do not be afraid to speak to some of the wrong doings going on in the community. But remember the proverb, that people living in a glass house should not be throwing stones.

"They are not of the world, just as I am not of the world" (John 17:16-17, NKJV).

You Are a City On a Hill

You cannot afford to hide in public, you are a city on a hill. You are the light and the salt of the world. Above all, you are a beacon of hope and glory to many in your community. This is how the community sees us and so we must honor it and comport ourselves with dignity, magnifying our ministries.

> "You are the light of the world. A city that is set on a hill cannot be hidden. Nor do they light a lamp and put it under a basket, but on a lampstand, and it gives light to all who are in the house" (Matt 5:14-15, NKJV).

Let me say this, my wife and I, lived at Ahafo Hwidiem in Ghana, where we gave birth and raised our five biological children. The Lord used us so much that we invested a lot of spirituality in people. When you invest in people, you never lose. Three years ago, I went to Ghana and to that same city for a program. The reception that was accorded my wife and I was like President Obama coming to Southside of Chicago. I mean, people were rushing to come and see us. It was amazing. Salvation to a soul is more than precious gold as confirmed by Mark 8:36 (For what shall it profit a man, if he shall gain the whole world, and lose his own soul? - a favorite Scripture verse of my "Spiritual Mentor," Evangelist Dr. Billy Graham.

> "And how does a man benefit if he gains the whole world and loses his soul in the process?" (Mark 8:36, TLB).

My brothers and sisters, ministry is a great and honorable work God has given us. It is not about money, intellectuality, degree, fame, but it is all about expanding God's Kingdom. So let us invest in people. These were young boys and girls I invested spiritually in, when I was a teacher. A teacher comes as an encouragement to us all. Whenever you see your spiritual fathers or your spiritual mothers you really want to do everything within your power to bless them. So that's exactly what was happening in Ghana.

Network with Other Minsters and Ministries

Ministerial networking is okay. Endeavor to network with other ministers and ministries like Trinity Broadcasting Network (TBN), the Word Network, and others. Prayerfully partner with those who enrich your life and ministry and not just anybody. I borrowed this idea from Bishop TD Jakes. I listen to him a lot, honestly. I like his wisdom and learn a lot from him.

Leave your palace and travel to other places and ministries to develop and enrich your ministerial horizon. Some people don't leave their church for any reason to see what God is doing in other places. I honor those who do. When you see greater things God is doing with others, you are positively challenged and provoked to expand the horizon of your thinking and ministry. That is how we grow. When you stop being challenged, you stop growing. Some people are so comfortable in their palaces, that they will never leave their palaces to see more glorious magnificent palaces. Make no mistake, it takes the spirit of humility and wisdom for a chief to leave his palace to go and serve in another palace. Yes, it does, think about that.

Conclusively, there is no clear cut dichotomy in the private, the professional, and the public lives of the pastor or leader. As a matter of fact, all three, despite theological attempt to distinct them, are intrinsically intertwined and interwoven. In other words, we cannot separate them. They are all interwoven.

CHAPTER 4

The Counseling And Support Needs Of The Pastor/Leader: Who Pastors The Pastor?

From the earlier chapters above, the reader can easily understand and appreciate the many challenges pastors and church leaders go through in their private, professional, and public lives. The pastor/leader is either a husband/father, wife/mother, son, daughter, or the head of an organization or community leader. The societal expectation of the pastor/leader is very high. The pastor/leader is expected to give an excellent account of himself/herself regardless of whatever. Let us be honest and realistic of the fact that the pastor/leader is human like the reader and has problems and challenges of life, and not superhuman. It takes the grace of God to respond to the calling upon our lives, and it is same grace through the inspiration of the Holy Spirit that enables us to lead God's people to the "Promised Land."

Human Weaknesses of the Pastor/Leader

The human weaknesses of Moses amplify the point in the foregone paragraph. From the day one of his calling, Moses gave all kinds of excuses of his inadequacies and human weaknesses. What God needs from us is our willingness and availability. When He sees that in our hearts, He enables us for the assignment ahead.

> "Moses said to the Lord, "Pardon your servant, Lord. I have never been eloquent, neither in the past nor since you have spoken to your servant. I am slow of speech and tongue" (Exod. 4:10, NIV).

The prophet Jeremiah expressed the same insufficiency and inadequacy when he was called by God. I am quoting the same text in Jeremiah 1:6 from different versions to portray how fearful Jeremiah was as he said the same thing differently:

> "Alas, Sovereign Lord," I said "I do not know how to speak; I am too young"-NIV

> "O Sovereign Lord, "I said, "I can't speak for you! I am too young!"- NLT

> Then I said, "Ah, Lord God! Behold, I do not know how to speak, for I am only a youth"-ESV

> Then I said, "Alas, Lord God! Behold, I do not know how to speak, Because I am a youth"-NASB

> Then said I, Ah Lord God! Behold, I cannot speak: for I am a child- KJV

The list can go on unending. The core point being expressed here is the fact that about 9/10 of ministers doubted and challenged their initial call. Some were doing very well in the corporate world before the call and therefore they could not fathom why they should leave and pursue a life of ministry with its countless challenges. Some assembled powerful men and women of God who had gone ahead of them in ministry to check the validity and the authenticity of God's call upon their lives. The reader in ministry can easily resonate with this point. Interestingly, the more they sought for confirmation, the clearer it became. Spiritual mentorship and counseling is very important at this stage in the life of the individual upcoming minister. Any ministry comes with the specifics as we ask these questions meditatively- when do I begin? Where do I start? Which ministry and who becomes my mentor? Moses mentored Aaron, prophet Elijah did same with Elisha, Apostle Paul and young Timothy, Kathryn Kuhlman and Pastor Benny Hinn, and many contemporary examples of God Fathers/Mothers and Sons/Daughters in ministry.

Locate Your Spiritual Mentor

God purposefully brings spiritual fathers/mothers and others in our lives for a specific reason. Some of the many abuses in ministry are traceable to the young minister's unwillingness to study at the feet of elderly/senior ministers. For three solid years the apostles studied at the feet of Jesus to equip themselves for future ministry. Being able to prophesy accurately or see clear visions does not make you a good minister. We must all go through the mill to reach the final product. The corn mill is a simple example, common to many African readers. As the fermented corn goes through the milling process, the machine literally cries with a loud noise and the corn's "silent cry" is unheard. The good news is that the final grounded corn becomes food for the family to enjoy. Gold shines and glitters but it starts off as a dirty black dust and through processing under extreme heated temperature, the final product is born. Just take a look at your beautiful wedding ring to appreciate and sympathize the mother gold that gave birth to the child-gold/ring.

We Grow Through Trials and Challenges

Challenges of life are not totally bad or evil in themselves. Trials in life and ministry make us totally dependent on God. To endure any form of trial you are going through now, is to be patient and keep on trusting the God who called you to lead his people.

> **"For you know that when your faith is tested, your endurance has a chance to grow" (Jam.1:3, NLT).**

James reminds us that our faith must be tested and through patience we endure to glorify God. Trial is an external challenge that comes your way not because of what you did wrong or did not do. The fundamental factor is faith –based. You are persecuted today because of your faith. You lost that job because you shared your faith at the workplace. My son, Dr. Mark Amoateng, arrived in the US during his medical school years and secured a very good job to pay for his air ticket and other expenses as a student. One day without any notice, he was instantly fired because he shared the love of Christ with a coworker. Some of you reading this book now can easily attest to this fact. Thanks be to God that in most African countries and other places in the world, it is not so. The love of Christ is shared freely. The gospel message though free, is expensive because Jesus shed His noble, precious, undefiled and expensive blood to eternally secure our pardon, redemption, and peace.

Do not confuse trial with temptation. Temptation is human-creation, that is, our flesh lures us into doing things contrary to our Christian faith and calling, and therefore, we suffer the consequences. This is not from God but the devil. James continues to tell/remind us that, temptation is from within.

> **"When tempted, no one should say, "God is tempting me." For God cannot be tempted by evil, nor does he tempt anyone but each person is tempted when they are dragged away by their own evil desire and enticed- (Jam. 1:13-14, NIV).**

To be able to handle trials and temptations in ministry successfully, you need to confide in an elderly/senior minister. At the end of the day, we are all prone to trials and temptations but the Holy Spirit is our enablement. Prayer support from prayer supporters and partners help us to endure and survive the storm (read more about prayer supporters and partners in my book titled *Spiritual Mentorship For Pastors and Church Leaders Today page 45*). The Apostle Paul having gone through trials and temptations turns round to encourage all Christians/ministers and says that **"bear one another's burdens, and so fulfil the law of Christ"- Gal. 6:2, KJV.** The burden mentioned here is generic- it can be a specific trial, temptation, a lack in finance, food, clothing, health, or other.

The Pastor/Leader is a Blessing to the Society

Our covenant relationship with God automatically confers on us the privilege to be a blessing to the society, especially as pastors/leaders in the Body of Christ. We must therefore endeavor to extend this blessing to our respective communities where our ministries are situated and teach our congregation to do likewise.

> "I, the Lord, have called You in righteousness, and will hold Your hand; I will keep You and give You as a covenant to the people, as a light to the Gentiles, to open blind eyes, to bring out prisoners from the prison, those who sit in darkness from the prison house" (Isa 42:6-7, NKJV).

However, the precondition to extend this inherent blessing to others is to allow God to take us through the breaking process. As you read the Scriptures below, you will notice that while the spikenard was still contained in the alabaster box, the impact of the fragrance was not felt by anyone in the room until it was released and poured out on Jesus. In the same vein, the blessing of God in our lives are dormant until they are released through the breaking process. Before Jesus gave the bread to His disciples both at the supper and to feed the multitude, He first **took** the bread, **blessed it** in prayer, **broke it** and then **gave it** to His disciples. All three Scriptures below attest to this principle.

> "And as they were eating, Jesus took bread, blessed and broke it, and gave it to the disciples and said, "Take, eat; this is My body" (Matt 26:26 NKJV).

> "Then Mary took a jar of costly perfume made from essence of nard, and anointed Jesus' feet with it and wiped them with her hair. And the house was filled with fragrance" (John 12:3, TLB).

> "Taking the five loaves and the two fish and looking up to heaven, he gave thanks and broke them. Then he gave them to the disciples to set before the people" (Luke 9:16-17, NIV).

Another metaphorical expression of this principle is the olive seed and the vine/grape. It takes the crushing of the olive seed to get the freshness of the anointing oil and the squashing of the vine/grape to get the sweetness of the wine. The olive seed holds the olive oil but through extraction, the oil is made available as a blessing to us. Like I have said earlier that process of getting the glittering gold from a dirty black dust is passing it through a streamlined rigorous process in the fire. The same also for that sparkling silver.

> **"He will sit as a refiner and a purifier of silver; He will purify the sons of Levi, and purge them as gold and silver, that they may offer to the Lord an offering in righteousness" (Mal 3:3, NKJV).**

This is the ultimate reason for the brokenness; that we may offer unto our God an offering of righteousness.

Marriage and Family Matters and Ministry

This sub-heading demands another chapter but time and space will not permit that. I am now attempting to hit the nail right on the head. Hitherto I was just hitting a side of the nail. Marriage is only second to our salvation in Christ. To be blessed with the right caring and loving spouse is indeed a real blessing. The opposite is equally true. Many have fallen from grace to grass because of marriage. I will highly recommend the book titled *The Right One: How to Successfully Date and Marry the Right Person* by Jimmy Evans and Frank Martin and Foreword by Kari Jobe for all the unmarried and also to the married pastors/leaders who counsel the youth. I wish to start off the discussion as I invite Apostle Paul to address the pastor/leader reading my book.

> **"But if a man does not know how to manage his own household, how will he take care of the church of God? - 1 Tim. 3:5, NASB.**

I appeal to anyone reading this book at this point to pause and reflect on the above quote from Apostle Paul.

Catholic theology refers to the family as the "domestic church." By this it means that if the domestic church is peaceful, progressive, respectful, and loving, it reflects on the larger church community. The many confusions in our churches today is a clear manifestation of what goes on at home in people's houses. No one needs a prophet to prophesy over this fact. The writings are loud and clear on the wall. Church members disrespect the pastor/leader because they do same at home to their husbands/wives/ fathers/mothers/sons/daughters, and other members in the family. The family that prays together, stays together. This is a spiritual truth and principle and the converse is also true. The first century Christians demonstrated it and worked for them. The 120 Family in the Upper Room prayed and stayed together as they supported each other. The support became more pronounced after the Ascension (Acts 1:6-11, Luke 24:50-53) and Pentecost (Acts 2:1-5) and thereafter in the book of Acts- Peter's imprisonment (Acts 12:5-17). Servant of God Father Patrick Peyton, C.S.C. (January 9, 1090-June 3, 1992) was an Irish Catholic priest, founder and promoter of the Post World War II prayer movement called, "Family Rosary Crusade." He was the originator of the spiritual saying that "the family that prays together says together."

Individual Roles in the Family in Relation to Ministry

The "Apostolic Exhortation" by Paul in Ephesians 5:21-33 on

Instructions for Christian Household distinctively spells out the role of each family member. There is no ambiguity in the "division of labor and roles" at all. Paul starts off with submission for all family members regardless of their status or position in life or ministry. He tells all wives to submit to their own husbands as unto the Lord for the simple reason that the husband is the head of the wife as Christ is the head of the church, his body, of which he is the savior. Paul continues to say that as the church submits to Christ, so also wives should submit to their husbands in everything. I want to leave Paul's instructions just as it is without entering into any "intellectual debate and argument." I know some wives have problem with Paul and question back to ask him what if the husband is not being responsible? Let each of us allow the Holy Spirit to speak to our hearts on this matter.

At this juncture, I wish to pause and salute all wives and mothers for the many things you do to keep the family going. The mother carries the baby for 9 months and thereafter begins compassionate and passionate caring and feeding of the baby; she is the manager of the "kitchen office" and manages effectively to feed all even with scarce resources. This is amazing.

In 1983, Ghana, my native country, experienced severe famine which resulted in the death of many but my wife, Mrs. Agatha Amoateng-Boahen ("Mama") made sure we had more to feed the immediate family and some Christian and non-Christian friends. The pastor's wife, affectionately referred to as the "First Lady" in some churches carries heavy responsibilities of maintaining her own house and also supporting her husband in ministry. The first lady plays many roles and wears many hats- the expectation of her is very high. But sorry to remark that the "office of the first lady" receives no formal training.

There is no school that trains the pastor's wife. I personally think we are just being unfair to them. How does the Chief Executive Officer (CEO) of a company expect the newly hired business executive from the University of Chicago Business School (one of the best business schools in the US) to perform excellently without giving him/her orientation? Some form of training/school is recommended for all pastors' wives to be able to meet the myriads of the roles they play in the family and church.

The fatherly role is as important as that of the mother. Many are biased against fathers and this evidenced by the extensive publicity for Mother's Day Celebration in the US and other countries. The number of cards sold is believed to be massive compared to those sold on Father's Day. Paul tells all fathers to love their wives as their own bodies and also reminds them if they have forgotten that they are the head of the family. Not just mere figure heads but "priests and pastors" of the home. The father among others, is the general overseer of the home, repairer of building, cars, and other appliances, manual and electrical. If the said father is also a pastor in ministry then the story assumes a greater responsibility and commitment. Fathers like mothers have done so much and we must honor and appreciate them. The challenges in certain cultures and communities are just too much to militate against fathers and all prospective fathers but with total dependence on God, prayer, and encouragement, we shall overcome. I now reecho the words in the Negro Spiritual by James Weldon Johnson titled "Lift Every Voice and Sing" for all fathers:

God of our weary years.
God of our silent tears.
Thou who hast brought us thus far on the way:

Thou who has by Thy might.
Led us into the light.
Keep us forever in the path, we pray.
Lest our feet stray from the places, our God, where we met Thee.
Lest our hearts, drunk with the wine of the world, we forget Thee:
Shadowed beneath Thy hand, may we forever stand.
Ture to our God, true to our native land.

Paul addresses all children to obey their parents because it is the first commandment that comes with a promise of blessings. Children, obey your parents in the Lord, for this is right.

"Honor your father and mother "- which is the first commandment with a promise- so that it may go well with you and that you may enjoy long life on the earth" (Gal. 6:1-3, NIV).

I can confidently say with a measure of accuracy and certainty that I obeyed my parents, who have transitioned to eternity, and all elders in the community growing up at Kintampo, Brong Ahafo, Ghana. I can also confirm that the accompanying promise is true, authentic, and validated in my own life. Children who are reading my book and also are pastors and ministers of the gospel, this is for your sober reflection and meditation because you cannot be too spiritual to disobey your parents. Please remember the African/Ghana proverb which says that "before the King was born, there were elders already living in the family house". Similarly, before you became a pastor/minister, your parents and other elders and leaders in the family and community were living. The pointer is to humility as a human and pastoral virtue. You cannot be too anointed to disrespect your elders and senior pastors and leaders in the church and community.

Finally, Paul exhorts both slaves and masters and passionately states:

> "Slaves, obey your earthly masters with respect and fear, and with sincerity of heart, just as you would obey Christ... because you know that the Lord will reward each one for whatever good they do, whether they are slave or free." And masters, treat your slaves in the same way. Do not threaten them, since you know that he who is both their Master and yours is in heaven, and there is no favoritism with him" (Gal. 6:5-9, NIV).

In the 21st century slavery in its orthodox form does not exist openly except in few countries. However, we can apply the above Scripture verses to the house masters/mistresses- house helps relationships of today. I mean the child care providers, health care providers who take care of the sick in homes, houseboys/men and girls/women, the drivers, the gardeners, the cooks, and all external helpers who depend on us for their daily bread and survival. This type of support is ministry in itself and we must therefore see it as the extension of the formal and recognizable church ministry.

Family Life is Integral and Cardinal to Effective Ministry

The man or woman of God cannot ignore family responsibilities and succeed in ministry. Let us all heed to the above apostolic exhortation by Paul to all Christians globally. Let us all join hands to build a beautiful and functional domestic church through prayer, Word study, respect, mutuality, and cooperation because the larger church community is a replica of the domestic church.

Business to Support Ministry and Accompanying Challenges

From the foregoing discussion, it can be argued and justified that the pastor/leader needs some sort of business or extra income to support family (bills, school fees for children, parental support at home, plans towards old age, and others) and also to support the ministry to alleviate the church from some of the heavily-loaded financial burdens and responsibilities. As cautioned earlier, the business must not replace the call of God upon your life. You can also not totally depend on the mercy of church support. Please listen to the Holy Spirit and beautifully and professionally embark on both. Money can impede or impact your ministry positively but you are encouraged to work the specifics out with the Holy Spirit in prayer.

Justification for the Pastor to Be Pastored

There is no clear cut dichotomy between each of the three aspects of the pastor's/leader's life. All three (private, professional, and public) aspects are argumentatively competitive and cumulative. The pastor/leader cannot do it all by oneself, and therefore, need support from the family, prayer supporters, prayer partners, church leaders, other ministers in the community, the church council or any professional associations if available. The pastor/leader must also engage the services of a professional counselor, psychotherapist, spiritual director, family doctor, or recreational therapist. Anything worth doing is worth doing well, and therefore, the pastor/leader must equally be willing to pay for the services of these professionals. From the above discussion in chapter 4, it can be justifiably concluded with a measure of accuracy that, the pastor/leader needs to be pastored by other professionals, family, fellow ministers, friends, prayer supporters, prayer partners, and others whenever the need arises- the question Who Pastors the Pastor is answered is answered and justified.

Conclusion

Having discussed this far on this subject, it is evident from the Scriptures that man as created by God is a tripartite being; comprising of the body, the soul, and the spirit, and he is expected to be fully functional in all three aspects.

> *"May God himself, the God of peace sanctify you through and through. May your whole spirit, soul, and body be kept blameless until our Lord Jesus Christ comes again" (I Thess. 5:23, NIV).*

This is Holistic Ministry. For the pastoral caregiver to be effective in his/her ministry, these three aspects of his/her life ought to be well-balanced and fully functional in all ramifications. His private, professional, and public lives are the vehicles through which he/she effectively administers care to people.

The pastor/leader must critically, patiently, and prayerfully listen and also create a sacred space and time for the counselee to identify the real need and must not conclude hastily for the client/church member/mentee/spiritual directee. Like the medical doctor, the pastor/leader patiently conducts the "spiritual laboratory investigation" to locate the real need as either physical/bodily, emotional/soul/mind, or spiritual. In certain instances, it can be one of the three, or two of the three, or all three needs- body, soul, and spirit- Holistic Ministry.

However, because of the high expectations society places on the pastor /leader, we fail to see the challenges they go through and the need for the pastoral caregiver to be pastored and cared for as well. From the previous chapters we can easily understand and appreciate the many challenges pastors and church leaders go through in their private, professional, and public lives. They are humans as we are, and not superhuman.

Because of the daunting task of leading God's people to the "Promised Land," it is imperative that by the help of the Holy Spirit, the pastor/leader be well developed in these three aspects of his/her life; the private, the professional, and the public life. The deliberate attempt made by the author to focus on the private, the professional, and the public lives of the pastoral caregiver - pastors, church leaders, chaplains, counselors, psychotherapists, clinical social workers, spiritual directors, health professionals, and others is to encourage and better equip the caregiver, thereby bridging the gap between the caregiver and the receiver/counselee, through effective pastoral care and holistic ministry.

Mrs. Agatha Amoateng-Boahen

Dr. Gabriel Amoateng-Boahen

Author's Profile

Dr. Gabriel Amoateng-Boahen was born to the Late Opanin Peter Kofi Amoateng (went to be with the Lord in February 1978) and the Late Maame Veronica Yaa Afrah (transitioned to Glory on March 19, 2013, thirty-five years after the death of my father) of Kintampo, Brong Ahafo, Ghana. He started school at the age of seven at the Bodom Presbyterian School and Effia Methodist Primary (near Effiakuma-Takoradi, the Port City). Gabriel returned to Kintampo in 1962 to continue his education at the Baffoe Local Authority and Middle Schools at Kintampo, where he was the Junior Prefect and Senior Prefect respectively (1962-1967; Gabriel's class was the first batch for the new school).

In 1967, Gabriel passed the Common Entrance Examination and gained admission to the Obuasi Secondary Technical School (1967-1972). From 1972-1974, Gabriel successfully completed his Post-Secondary Teacher Training College at Berekum, Brong Ahafo, and was posted to Ahafo Kenyasi II Catholic Primary School. A few weeks later, he was transferred to Ahafo Hwidiem Catholic Primary School, where Gabriel taught from 1974-1984 (part of divine plan unfolding –Jer.29:11).

Gabriel studied privately and passed the Advanced Level Examination and gained admission to pursue his undergraduate studies at the University of Science and Technology (now Kwame Nkrumah University of Science and Technology-KNUST) in Kumasi-Ghana from 1984-1987 and obtained his Bachelor of Arts in Social Sciences (final thesis "Comparative Study of Traditional and Church Marriages in the Brong Ahafo Region: A Case Study of the Hwidiem Traditional Area," UST, Kumasi-Ghana, 1987). From 1987-1989, Gabriel did the mandatory national service at the newly established Community Improvement Unit (CIU) at the Konongo District Office. Gabriel had a "desert experience" from 1990-1991 as he discerned God's plan for his life and also volunteered at the "infant" Maranatha Clinic (now Maranatha Hospital at Kwadaso/Asuoyeboa-Kumasi).

Gabriel was the Diocesan Development Coordinator for the Sunyani Catholic Diocese in 1991 and later became the headmaster for the St. Louis Junior Secondary School at Mbrom-Kumasi from 1992-1994. On May 6, 1995, he became the first-ever headmaster and co-founder of the Maranatha International School (now Maranatha Young Apostles) at Daban Panin-Kumasi. This school was established on sound Christian principles with the motto "Holistic Child Development" to demonstrate the harmonious interplay among hand, head, and heart (hand/body/physical, head/mind/soul/, and heart/the spirit of the human person- 1 Thess.5:23). Prov.9:10 and Prov. 22:6 were our key biblical verses, and both staff and students lived by the precepts of God's Word.

Gabriel arrived in New York on May 31, 2001, to pursue Clinical Pastoral Education (CPE) at the Hospital of Saint Raphael in

New Haven, Connecticut, USA, to be trained as a Chaplain, and thereafter proceeded to the Catholic Theological Union (CTU) in Chicago, Illinois, USA, for the Master of Arts in Pastoral Studies (MAPS) from 2002-2004 and the Ecumenical Doctor of Ministry degree from 2004-2007. Gabriel is a Certified Professional Chaplain (Retired) at the University of Chicago Medical Center and also the President and Founder of the Royal Diadem Pastoral Center in Chicago and Kumasi-Ghana.

Gabriel had a personal encounter and relationship with the Lord Jesus Christ on June 6, 1972, and ever since that time, has remained resolute and uncompromising with his Christian faith and has great passion for soul-winning. Gabriel has varied ministerial experiences. He was a member of the Scripture Union, Ghana (especially in the Ahafo and Sunyani areas), from 1974-1984; and he was the church secretary for the Holy Spirit Catholic Church at Ahafo Hwidiem. During that same period, he was the founder and first-ever secretary for the Ahafo Hwidiem Christian Fellowship and was also actively involved in the Council of Churches. Gabriel was the secretary of the first-ever Ghana Catholic School of Evangelization organized by the Germany and Malta teams and hosted by the Metropolitan Archdiocese of Kumasi-Ghana in 1992.

At the Catholic Charismatic Renewal front, Gabriel was a founding member of Mission 2000 (established on November 3, 1991), a Catholic Charismatic Renewal Prayer Group with focus on evangelizing Catholic adults and professionals. He is the current coordinator of the Charismatic Renewal at Our Lady of Sorrows Basilica at 3121 W. Jackson Boulevard in Chicago, and also a member of the Ghanaian Catholic Charismatic Renewal –North America

(G-CCR-NA) Leadership Coordinating Team (LCT) (appointed director for missions in June 2013 at the first-ever National Biennial Convention in Virginia). Gabriel is a founding member of the Ghanaian Catholic Community of Chicago and also the founder and coordinator of the Prayer Conference for the Catholic Community as well as the Christian Leaders for Tomorrow (CL4T) Prayer Conference- youth focused with Daniel 11:32b as its theme verse: "They that know their God shall be strong and do exploits." He is the "marriage counselor" for the local Catholic Community of Chicago and also for some Ghanaians in Chicago.

Gabriel is the Chaplain for the Brong Ahafo Association of Chicago and the keynote speaker at the Council of Brong Ahafo Associations of North America (COBAANA) in 2011; and he is also the Ombudsman for COBAANA. Gabriel has strong ecumenical inclination and is deeply involved in the activities of the Council of Ghanaian Churches in Chicago, where he is the current Vice President. Gabriel takes a lot of inspiration from Evangelist Dr. Billy Graham. He is Gabriel's "spiritual mentor" and has twice attended the Billy Graham Schools of Evangelism in Cincinnati, Ohio (2002), and Kansas City, Missouri (2004). Gabriel was at the Haggai Institute in Singapore in 2000 for the Advanced Leadership Training for Christian Leaders from Developing Countries.

He is a member of these professional associations: National Association of Catholic Chaplains (NACC), Association of Professional Chaplains (APC), Spiritual Direction International (SDI) and others. Gabriel was the representative for the University of Chicago Medical Center at the Kenwood-Hyde Park Interfaith Council (2010 - to May 31, 2015).

On March 27, 1977, Gabriel and Mrs. Agatha Amoateng-Boahen were joined together in holy matrimony at the Holy Spirit Catholic Church at Ahafo Hwidiem. They now live peacefully and happily with their eight children: Mrs. Veronica Amoateng Antwi; Rev. Sampson Amoateng; Rev. Mark Amoateng, MD; Rev. Daniel Amoateng; Rev. Brian Amoateng; Christabel Jessica Amoateng; Davina Amoateng; and Gabriel Amoateng Badu, Jr.

CONFERENCES, SEMINARS, AND CONTINUOUS EDUCATION

All Pastors and Leaders Conference (APALEC), Stratford Christian Center Church, Chicago, Illinois, USA, 2016.

Ghanaian Catholic Charismatic Renewal –North America (G-CCR-NA), Second Biennial Convention, Bronx, New York, USA, 2015.

All Pastors and Leaders Conference (APALEC), House of Miracles, Medina Estates, Accra-Ghana, 2015.

Ghana Catholic Charismatic Renewal (National Outreach Leaders) Conference, Adom Fie-Kumasi, 2015.

Council of Brong Ahafo Associations of North America (COBAANA) Convention, Bronx, New York, USA, 2014.

Diversity and Inclusion Competency, University of Chicago Medicine, Illinois, USA, Fall 2014.

Ghanaian Catholic Charismatic Renewal –North America (G-CCR-NA), First-Ever Biennial Convention, Falls Church, Virginia, USA, 2013.
Council of Brong Ahafo Associations of North America (COBAANA) Convention, Washington DC, USA, 2013.

All Pastors and Leaders Conference (APALEC), House of Miracles, Medina Estates, Accra-Ghana, 2013.

All Pastors and Leaders Conference (APALEC), Life Community Chapel, Kumasi-Ghana, 2013.
Council of Brong Ahafo Associations of North America (COBAANA) Convention, Columbus, Ohio, USA, 2012.

Council of Brong Ahafo Associations of North America (COBAANA) Convention, Chicago, Illinois, USA, 2011.

All Pastors and Leaders Conference (APALEC), House of Miracles, Medina Estates, Accra-Ghana, 2010.

Council of Brong Ahafo Associations of North America (COBAANA) Convention, Toronto, Canada, 2010.

Kwame Nkrumah University of Science and Technology (KNUST) Alumni National Conference, Chicago, Illinois, USA, 2010.

National Association of Catholic Chaplains' Conference, Columbus, Ohio, USA, 2006.

Benny Hinn Miracle Crusade, Milwaukee, Wisconsin, USA, 2004.

Billy Graham School of Evangelism, Kansas City, Missouri, USA, 2004.
Archdiocese of Chicago Charismatic Renewal Conference, Chicago, Illinois, USA, 2003.

Trained Volunteer Tutor at Laubach Literacy Action, Chicago, Illinois, USA, 2003.

Benny Hinn Miracle Crusade, Louisville, Kentucky, USA, 2002.

Billy Graham School of Evangelism, Cincinnati, Ohio, USA, 2002.
Investment in Africa Conference, Worcester, Massachusetts, USA, 2002.

Connecticut American Montessori Conference, Hartford, Connecticut, USA, 2002.

National Catholic Charismatic Renewal Conference, Scranton, Pennsylvania, USA, 2002.

National American Montessori Conference, Atlanta, Georgia, USA, 2001.

Advanced Leadership Training for Christian Leaders in Developing Countries, Singapore, Asia, 2000.

Catholic Charismatic Renewal Leaders' Conference, Kumasi-Ghana, 2000.

Berekum Training College Old Students Association (BETCOSA), Kumasi-Ghana, 2000.

First-Ever Ghana Catholic School of Evangelization by Germany and Malta Teams, Kumasi-Ghana, 1992.

Ghana Scripture Union /Christian Fellowship (Ecumenical) - Retreats, Crusades, Camp Meetings, and Conferences (Ahafo Hwidem, Goaso, Sunyani, and Kumasi), 1975-1988.

EDUCATION

2004-2007: Catholic Theological Union (CTU), Chicago, Illinois, USA; Ecumenical Doctor of Ministry.

2005-2006: Claret Center, Chicago, Illinois, USA; Spiritual Direction International Internship.

2002-2004: Catholic Theological Union (CTU), Chicago, Illinois, USA; Master of Arts in Pastoral Studies (MAPS).

2001-2002: Clinical Pastoral Education (CPE) Residency, Saint Raphael Hospital, New Haven, Connecticut, USA.

1984-1987: Kwame Nkrumah University of Science and Technology (KNUST), Kumasi-Ghana, Bachelor of Arts (Social Sciences).

1972-1974: Berekum Post-Secondary Teacher Training College, Berekum, Brong Ahafo Region, Ghana.

1967-1972: Obuasi Secondary Technical (SECTECH) Obuasi, Ashanti Region, Ghana.
1960-1962: Kintampo Local Authority Primary and Middle Schools, Kintampo, Brong Ahafo Region, Ghana

1960-1962: Effia Methodist Primary School, Effia (Near Effiekuma, Takoradi Port City), Western Region, Ghana.

1959-1960: Bodom Presbyterian Primary School, Bodom-Nkoranza, Brong Ahafo Region, Ghana.

EMPLOYMENT HISTORY

2005-2015: Board Certified Professional Staff Chaplain, University of Chicago Medical Center, Chicago, Illinois, USA.

2014-2016: Ombudsman, Council of Brong Ahafo Associations of North America (COBAANA).

2013-2016: Missions Director, Ghanaian Catholic Charismatic Renewal- North America (G-CCRA-NA).

2010-2015: Representative of University of Chicago Medical Center at the Kenwood-Hyde Park Interfaith Council, Chicago, Illinois, USA.

August-November 2005: Staff Chaplain, Mercy Hospital, Chicago, Illinois, USA.

2003-2005: Registry Chaplain, University of Chicago Hospitals, Chicago, Illinois, USA.

1995-2001: Headmaster, Maranatha International School, Daban Panin-Kumasi, Ashanti Region, Ghana.

1991-1993: Headmaster, St. Louis Junior Secondary School, Mbrom-Kumasi, Ashanti Region, Ghana.

1990-1991: Diocesan Development Officer, Sunyani Catholic Diocese, Sunyani, Brong Ahafo Region, Ghana.

1974-1984: Headteacher, Catholic Primary School, Hwidiem, Brong Ahafo Region, Ghana.

1974, September-October: Teacher, Catholic Primary School, Ahafo Kenyasi II, Brong Ahafo Region, Ghana.

1974-2016: Counselor and Spiritual Director & Chaplain, Evangelist/Preacher/Conference Speaker, Volunteer Church Worker in Parishes, Churches, and Ministries.

Author's Profile

DONATIONS

Donations Accepted at http://donations.ghanarodi.org
Website: *www.ghanarodi.org*

E-Mail: *gabriel@ghanarodi.org*

gabriel.ab925@yahoo.com

gabrielabm1913@gmail.com

Chicago: Tel: 773-968-1983, 773-363-7889

Ghana: Tel: 020-812-1463, 020-783-0406, 020-783-0000

TO ORDER COPIES OF MY BOOKS IN CHICAGO

Kilimanjaro International, Hyde Park

1305 East 53rd Street

Chicago, IL 60615

Tel: 773-324- 4860

Email: katumba2@alive.com

Xlibris Publishers

1-888-795-4274

TO ORDER COPIES OF MY BOOKS ONLINE

Orders@Xlibris.com

www.Xlibris.com

www.amazon.com

www.barnesandboble.com

Available Formats: EBook, Audio Book, Paper and Hard Cover.

REHOBOTH HOUSE ONLINE DISTRIBUTORS

www.amazon.com

https://www.eden.co.uk

http://www.powells.com

http://www.audible.com

www.barnesandboble.com

http://www.christianbook.com

http://www.booksamillion.com/books

http://www.deepershopping.com/books.html

Available Formats: EBook, Audio Book, Paper and Hard Cover.

Recommended Books for Further Professional And Spiritual Development

1. *Integral Pastoral Care in Ghana: Proposals for Healing in the Asante Context* by Gabriel Amoateng-Boahen.
2. *The "Culture of Silence" Contributes to Perpetuating Domestic Violence: A Case Study of Family Life in the Brong Ahafo Region of Ghana* by Gabriel Amoateng-Boahen.
3. *Spiritual Mentorship for Pastors and Church Leaders Today* by Gabriel Amoateng-Boahen.
4. *My Ministry is Where My Misery Was* by Gabriel Amoateng- Boahen.
5. *Testimonies Today Tributes Tomorrow* by Gabriel Amoateng-Boahen.
6. *Pastoral Care and Holistic Ministry* by Gabriel Amoateng-Boahen.
7. *The Controlling Power Of The Mind: Renewing Your Mind Unto Victory* by Gabriel Amoateng-Boahen.
8. *African Punctuality: Time Is Divine And Of The Greatest Essence.*
9. by Gabriel Amoateng-Boahen.
10. *Spiritual Labour Room: Travailing Prayer* by Veronica Amoateng Antwi.
11. *Guarding and Protecting Your Prophetic Word* by Daniel Amoateng.
12. *Dreams and Their Interpretations* by Daniel & Brian Amoateng.
13. *From Impossibilities to Possibilities* by Daniel Amoateng.
14. *500 Wise Words and Life Lessons* by Daniel Amoateng.

Recommended Books for Further Professional And Spiritual Development

13. *Daily Prophetic Declarations* by Daniel Amoateng.
14. *Exposing Dream Killers* by Daniel Amoateng.
15. *Why Was I Born?* by Daniel Amoateng.
16. *Favour* by Brian Amoateng.
17. *100 Wisdom Tablets* by Brian Amoateng.
18. *Hindrances to Prayer* by Brian Amoateng.
19. *5 Mistakes to Avoid in Life* by Brian Amoateng.
20. *You Can Recover From a Fall* by Brian Amoateng.
21. *Walking in the Favour of God* by Brian Amoateng.
22. *Dreams and Their Interpretations* by Brian Amoateng.
23. *Favor, Your key to Lasting Success* by Brian Amoateng.
24. *Answers God Gives When We Pray* by Brian Amoateng.
25. *Keys to Effective Travelling Ministry* by Brian Amoateng.
26. *The Wonders of Speaking in Tongues* by Mark Amoateng.
27. *How to Receive from God* by Mark Amoateng.
28. *The Law of Seed by* Sampson Amoateng.
29. *Possessing the Kingdom* by Jesse Sackey.
30. *Understanding the Divine Timing of God* by Victor Owusu-Teng.
31. *Understanding Your Divine Calling & Purpose by* Victor Owusu-Teng.
32. *Mission–Minded Skits* by Cynthia Miller.
33. *Mission-Minded Skits* by Cynthia Miller.
34. *Practical Psychology for Pastors* by William R. Miller.
35. *Called to Care: A Christian Theology of Nursing* by Arlene B. Miller.
36. *Restoring Fallen Pastors* by Eric Reed.
37. *Beyond Suffering* by Joni Eareckson Tada.
38. *Pastoral: An Essential Guide* by John Patton.

39. *Prayer: The 30 Most Powerful* by John Bernthal.
40. *The Strategically Small Church* by Brandon O'Brien.
41. *Leadership: Be Humble, Stay Hungry* by Brad Lomenick.
42. *Personal Identity in Theological Perspective* by Richard Lints.
43. *Dangerous Calling: Confronting the Unique* by Paul David Tripp.
44. *48. In the Name of Jesus Reflections* by Henri J. M. Nouwen.
45. *The Emotionally Healthy Leader: How to Leader* by Peter Scazzero.
46. *Pastoral Care in Context: An Introduction to Pastoral Care* by John Patton.
47. *Being a Pastor: Understanding Our calling and Work* by Derek J. Prime.
48. *Ministerial Ethics: Moral Formation for Church Leaders* by Joe E. Trull.
49. *Fivefold Ministry Made practical: How to Release Apostles, Prophets, Evangelists, Pastors, and Teachers to Equip Today's Church* by Ron Myer.
50. *The Right One: How to Successfully Date and Marry the Right Person* by Jimmy Evans and Frank Martin.
51. *Is God Calling Me?: Answering the Question Every Leader Believer Asks* by Jeff Lorg.
52. *Brothers, We Are Not Professionals: A Plea to Pastors for Radical Ministry* by John Piper.
53. *Be Thou Prepared: Equipping the Church for Persecution and Times of Trouble* by Carl Gallups.
54. *Practical Wisdom for Pastors: Words of Encouragement and Counsel for a Lifetime* by Curtis C. Thomas.
55. *Mentoring Leaders: Wisdom for Developing Character, Calling, and Competency* by Carson Pue.
56. *Preaching: Communicating Faith in an Era of Skepticism* by Timothy Keller.

Recommended Books for Further Professional And Spiritual Development

57. *The Wounded Healer: Ministry in Contemporary Society* by Henri J.M. Nouwen.
58. *Pastoral Bearings: Lived Religion and Pastoral Theology* by Leonard Hammel.
59. *Professional Spiritual and Pastoral Care: A Practical Clergy and Chaplains' Handbook.*

PRAYER

Acceptance, Rededication, Recommitment, And Refire

Salvation:
Prayer to accept Jesus Christ as Lord and Savior (ABCD of Salvation)

A—Admit in humility that you are a sinner (Romans 3:23).
B—Believe on the Lord Jesus Christ, and thou shall be saved, and thy house (Acts 16:31).
C—Confess with your mouth the Lord Jesus and believe in your heart that God has raised him from the dead, you will be saved (Rom. 10:9).
D—Dedicate your body to Christ henceforth (Rom 12:1).

Repeat the prayer after me:
Lord Jesus, I have heard your word today. I admit that I am a sinner. I confess to you all my sins, known and unknown. Forgive me because I have greatly sinned against you. I accept you as my personal Lord and Savior. Come into my heart; take full control of my life. I hand over the key of my life to you. Take me and make me thy own henceforth. Amen!

If you prayed and believed the prayer, then John 1:12 is for you.

"...But as many as received him, to them gave he power to become the sons of God, even to them that believe on his name" (John 1:12).

REDEDICATION/RECOMMITMENT

"Revive Me, O Lord" (Psalm 119:156)

Please offer this Prayer of Rededication to the Lord:
"Revive me, O Lord" (Ps. 119:156).

"Restore unto me the joy of your salvation, and grant me a willing spirit, to sustain me" (Ps. 51:12).

"Now the Lord is the Spirit, and where the Spirit of the Lord is, there is freedom" (2 Cor. 3:17).

Prayer by author for reader:
Gracious and everlasting God, through the inspiration and power of the Holy Spirit, I pray with the reader right now. Please, Lord, rekindle the individual's spirit with your love and peace, and rejuvenate your child and restore your illumination and enlightenment to the yearning soul. In Jesus' Name. Amen!

FOR ALL "ON FIRE" BRETHREN

Retreat! Retire! And Refire!

Prayer:
Come, Holy Spirit, to reenergize me for service!
Let me experience another Pentecost,
A new personal Pentecost in my life!
I receive the new Pentecost fire by faith! Amen!

www.ingramcontent.com/pod-product-compliance
Lightning Source LLC
Chambersburg PA
CBHW060536080526
44586CB00012B/756